NURTURING YOUR WEALTH TRANSFER

(Late) Keith Dean and Larriett Josey Dean

ISBN:
978-1-966968-40-5 (eBook)
978-1-966968-39-9 (Paperback)

Published by:

OWL® PUBLISHERS

www.owlpublishers.com
360 S Market St, San Jose, CA 95113,
United States.

DEDICATED TO

All persons seeking to honestly obtain lasting Wealth.

ACKNOWLEDGMENTS

I wish to acknowledge the Mr. Late Keith Dean for his contribution to this book.

You Have the Power

Manuscript

"And Ye Shall Spoil The Egyptians…" Exodus 3:22

ABSTRACT

Nurturing your Wealth Transfer a faith based book, with practical applications. Not strictly religious nor strictly economic or business oriented. It utilizes a Pentateuch, a Judeo-Christian biblical foundation, to build a case for how an individual, despite disadvantages and trying life circumstances, can overcome poverty or the middle class trap to become truly economically independent.

This book is designed for those in or approaching mid-life who though having worked for years, earned College and University qualifications, worked for fortune 500 companies, are faced with foreclosure, layoffs, economic stagnation, loss of middle class status and general living from paycheck to paycheck.

The demographic for this book will thus be faith believing, middle class existing Generation X'ers. These Generation X'ers are fifty million (50,000,000) strong in North America. This was the generation that was supposed to "have it all". However, many Gen Xers find themselves struggling in a 21st century economy which seems to be trying to skip and squeeze them out.

You as the reader of Initiating Your Wealth Transfer book will discover biblical and Practical principles that can help you navigate the traps of poverty and a false middle class lifestyle, to truly discover real, long lasting wealth.

You will find that education, training, and positive thinking really have little influence on whether one remains in poverty or becomes wealthy during his/her lifetime. Wealth is a process of transfer. Many remain poor because they miss opportunities to demand the system to transfer their God given wealth.

The book will seek explanations as to why many people (Even Faith based Believers) remain poor, despite having the power to get wealth. In addition, the book examines the root cause of lifelong and intergenerational poverty. Some of these reasons will be seen as not recognizing opportunity; the lack of a wealth generating system; and the lack of a strong spiritual connection to the creator, who has wired us for wealth. Other reasons may be challenges with personal corruption and not understanding one's own intellectual capital.

Typical self-help books will be seen as lacking practical application. Why some people are poor in a rich and wealthy land, examines poverty from a wider perspective. The experiences learned in poverty can be used as a stepping stone to wealth creation and maintenance.

If you believe in God The Heavenly Father (Father Yahweh), you are entitled to your wealth transfer by one of two (2) means:

1. Solving a problem facing Egypt (your community, or nation) as in biblical character Joseph (son of Israel).

2. Placing a demand on Egypt Moses and The children of Israel).

The book explores common themes found in The Torah and The Bible, which surround the ancient superpower, and cradle of western civilization known as Egypt. While the book does not seek to have readers literally explore The Egyptian ancient command economy to find twenty first century wealth possibilities, the principles for wealth accumulation remain the same throughout the ages.

Table of Content

CHAPTER ONE: BEING POOR IN A RICH AND WEALTHY LAND

Following the 2008 world financial crisis, many people went through economic doldrums. Prior to this crisis, jobs which were said to be traditionally stable, went out of the window. Many new job seekers in the marketplace, fresh out of college, would wait months, even years for a solid prospect.

Many people who assumed that they were in a state of being called "The Middle Class", suddenly realized that they were facing something called poverty for the first time in their lives. Many, unable to pay their mortgages, found that the financial institutions holding the mortgage notes began foreclosing.

The foundation of wealth for many in North America, was the value of equity they held in their dwelling homes. This soon became to be seen for what it was, a faulty hope. It was this very foundation that many people held onto, which in fact was a root cause of much of the financial turmoil in the markets.

What then is poverty?

When we in Western society have thought about what it means to be poor, several different types of images are conjured up in our minds. We may see the image of a small child, with a large round pot belly, with an empty bowl in his hand. We may think about an old hobo, with a Johnny bundle sac, sleeping in a cardboard box, underneath an overpass intersection in a busy city. Other images which may come to mind, is a mother, walking into Walgreens Pharmacy, with a baby in a carrier, along with two older children, as she takes government food stamps to the cashier, with a shopping cart of grocery items.

Perhaps these traditional images can be seen as what poverty is. Certainly the persons mentioned above comprise a portion of the poor class. Yes, such persons do face financial and physical hardship associated with being poor. But, is poverty just the mere appearance of an absolute lack of physical resources? Is it just a lack of education or illiteracy in some instances? Is it simply not being able to enjoy common pleasures, such as not being able to take a wife to dinner on her birthday or anniversary, or giving children presents on their birthday? Or not being able to afford to acquire or maintain an automobile?

Poverty has a much wider scope of implications, and has a much greater group of people in its grips than we may have ever thought possible.

According to Time.com,

(www.business.time.com/2013/07/24/whatitmeanstobewealthyina mericatoday) less than one percent (1%) of Americans can claim the following to be true of their financial situation:

"I do have an emergency fund that can cover at least three (3) months of expenses in the event of an unforeseen disaster."

The simple truth is most of us are really living just one step away from abject poverty if we accept that the above statement represents a cut off line between the truly well off and the poor. Disasters and unforeseen catastrophic events such as Hurricane Katrina, and the 2008 financial meltdown, have a way of showing who really is the rich and the poor.

Sure, we can say that our federal government will not allow us to ultimately come down to nothing, because today's governments are inclined to give massive bailouts to its people from the public purse to avert complete disaster. But, that is not the issue of which we are now discussing. People depend on the government every day for their livelihood and sustenance. To qualify for such benefits, you must officially be classified by government agencies as, that's right, 'poor' in many instances.

Poverty has a face, and that face may really be more familiar than we think. The definition of poverty thus, for purposes of this book is;

"Anyone in a rich society, who is unable to afford an emergency fund to cover at least three months of expenses in the event of an unforeseen or catastrophic event."

In other words, if you were laid off from your job today, can you sustain yourself for a minimum of three (3) months without totally drastic changes to your lifestyle and pattern of living? Most of us in Generation X, cannot make that claim. We are really and essentially living at the doorstep of poverty.

Indeed, many of us can be classified as "the working poor". We have jobs in some instances which provide us with a measure of satisfaction about how we feel about ourselves. But we are really slaves to our jobs, our bosses, our Mortgage Company or bank. The bible indicates that "The Lender is the Master of The Borrower."

Our credit cards are maxed out; our car notes are in arrears; our checking accounts are in overdraft; we are paying back high interest rate student loans with no end in sight to principal payments for years on the horizon.

Many of us Generation X'ers are delaying having families and children for years into the future, for we see no way of comfortably affording marriage, and child rearing. Some of us are content to, "Do badly all by ourselves".

Movies and films are being released, admonishing our generation to adopt this attitude. Generation X is the first Generation that is not doing as well or better financially than its parents.

This is all because we refuse to come to grips with reality. Most of us are a part of the working poor. We are able to afford simple pleasures. A downtown studio apartment; a small house in the suburbs; Having lunch at a downtown bistro; going to the theater to watch a Broadway musical;

earning a college degree, and even perhaps doing postgraduate studies. We can walk onto a "zero down, zero interest, zero payments" auto dealership and "sign and drive". But, if we get laid off, we must immediately join Uncle Sam's welfare line.

This chapter explores who really is poor in North America today, along with the implications of poverty.

CHAPTER TWO: "IS HAVING GREAT WEALTH SINFUL?"

Many have traditionally held the belief that being wealthy is sinful. They in fact use "The Judeo Christian Bible" to justify this belief. It is true that The Bible admonishes against the accumulation of possessions for the sake of accumulating possessions, with greed as the prime motive. Is it true that you are in greater danger of hellfire if you have wealth?

"Is being wealthy sinful?" examines biblical truths about wealth, along with characters who were wealthy, yet did not allow abundant possessions and resources to deceive them into a false sense of immortality and security. They served their Creator through wealth and did not become carried away by it. Such Characters include but are not limited to, Abraham, Isaac, Jacob, Joseph, King David, Queen Esther, King Solomon, Job, Joseph of Arimathea, etc. Modern non biblical characters in the public domain such as Bill Gates, Warren Buffet, Shek Khan and Lee Chin will also be examined. For though some of them may profess no outward faith in The Heavenly Father, most recognize his principles for obtaining and managing wealth.

There is a misconception held by some that poverty is a better state of being spiritually. The Beatitudes and Jesus' (Yashua's), "Camel through the eye of a needle" retort to the rich young ruler seems to justify the myth. Jesus' parable about "The Rich Fool", as well as Paul's "Money is the source of all kinds of evil" comment in the new testament, seem to suggest to many that having monetary assets and possessions is inherently evil, and will lead the possessor to an eventual after life of eternal damnation.

Both Jesus (Yahsua) and The Apostle Paul (formerly Saul) admonish the accumulation of "riches" as being evil, not honestly earned wealth. Jesus himself spoke favorably of wealth in the parable of the talents, and in fact bemoaned the foolish servant, who thinking he was rich, tried to hide the talent from attracting wealth. Jesus referred to this non risk taking servant in fact as evil. Jesus uses the illustration to show the wealthy landlord who returned from a far country to bring his servants into account for their stewardship over his wealth not as evil, but as righteous.

In the above parable, the foolish servant, rather than using what was granted to him to benefit the Master's objectives, became consumed with what he perceived as an inferior position as compared with his fellow servants. This servant felt the need to horde the possession he had custody over, and envy those with.

We see above that The Heavenly Father gives His servants the POWER to obtain wealth. Why would God grant a power to his child that was basically sinful in nature?

God, however, does have the power to delay wealth transfers, until he deems that we are spiritually ready to handle it.

Certainly, the wealth of Abraham, Isaac and Jacob, the children of Israel under Moses, the wealth of Egypt as transferred to Vizier Joseph, King David, Solomon (who built the Temple), Job (the wealthiest man in all the east), King Hezekiah, Queen Esther, and the wealth transfer to Nehemiah to rebuild Jerusalem, along with that of Joseph of Arimathea (who bought Jesus' tomb), can hardly be deemed as sinful.

CHAPTER THREE: WEALTH VERSUS RICHES

In this chapter, we compare and contrast wealth versus riches. Accumulation of riches will be seen from a biblical and worldly perspective as being a selfish, vain activity that is unsustainable in the long run. The rich today, poor tomorrow syndrome can be seen in such persons as some sports personalities, music icons, and lottery ticket winners, who win big today, but lose countless millions tomorrow. Accumulation of wealth will be seen as a natural spin-off of seizing honest opportunities presented which can maximize your talent, at the right time and season.

We must begin by debunking myths that most people hold. The prime myth is that the terms wealth and riches are synonymous. An individual can be very rich but not wealthy. Meaning, that a person can have lots of access to money, possessions, and resources for a period of time, but may not necessarily be wealthy.

A rich man can have a poor sense of values, judgment, vision, sensitivity to the needs of others, knowledge of handling finances, and be in poor physical, spiritual and emotional health.

By extension, a wealthy person has both possessions along with a healthy state of being. Such an individual experiences life in its fullest form. Christ described this as his reason for coming to earth. Of his coming to earth, Christ (Yashua) speaks of spiritual, emotional, physical health and wellbeing as follows:

"I come that they might have life and that they might have it more abundantly." (John Chapter 10:10, Zondervan KJV, page 2170)Certainly, Christ (Yahshua) came to die for our sins, and give us eternal life. But here in John 10, he demonstrates that he desires that we live abundantly here on earth as well. His prerequisite for this life of wealth however is this:

"Seek ye first The Kingdom of God and his righteousness, and all these things shall be added unto you."

(Matthew 6:33, Zondervan KJV, page 1947)

The key thing with being wealthy is that the wealthy understand where the true source of their wealth lies. It's in pursuing God's agenda, and his will, without question and absolutely.

It is those with a rich man's mentality who in fact;

"Lay up treasures on Earth, where moth and rust doth corrupt, and where thieves break in and steal."

(Matthew 6:19, Zondervan KJV page 1947)

This does not of course mean that the wealthy individual is "broke" of possessions. The wealthy person's heart does not worship these possessions, or find security in them as in the "rich man's strong city". The wealthy do not define their worth in "the abundance of things they possess".

The wealthy have a balanced life, and stand ready to give away possessions, should he/she be called upon to do so by The Heavenly Father, as Abraham was prepared to do with Isaac.

The rich define themselves exclusively by their worldly possessions. The "Rich Fool", for instance, took comfort and self-worth in his goods and possessions which were stored up for many years.

The wealthy allow God (Yahweh) to define them in accordance with his will. God said of the greatest (and wealthiest) man of the east, Job;

"Hast thou considered my servant Job, that there is none like him in the earth,

A perfect and upright man, one that feareth God, and eschewed (abhors, avoids) Evil?" (Job 2, Zondervan KJV)

The job was not even around when God defined him as righteous. Job is a prime example of what wealth means to the Believer. Of Job, The bible says that he was,

".one that feared God"

(Job, 1:1, Zondervan KJV, page 982)

Job's wealth consisted of spiritual well being, intellectual capital, emotional wellbeing, and physical wellbeing along with great substance or possessions. The Book of Job (Zondervan KJV, page 982) says of Job's substance and very great household that;

"...so that this man was the greatest (and wealthiest) of all men of the east"

Wealth in those days and even in some regions today, was defined by livestock. In some countries in the twenty first century, having a lone family goat represents a form of wealth, for the goat produces milk, which can be sold.

In comparing and contrasting the rich versus the wealthy, we will see that rich men/women can be well off for a portion of their lives or for a lifetime. Wealthy men, on the other hand, are prosperous for generations (as Abraham's seed is).

Being rich will be seen as a shortsighted endeavor, which benefits a small scope of individuals. One can be a "poor old rich man", who never truly experiences true wealth, prosperity, and happiness. The rich man finds peace and comfort in greed. His greed eventually becomes his downfall.

This is sort of like the analogy of the dog and the bone. A dog, having a tender, juicy bone in its mouth, looks into a pond of water. Upon looking into the water, he discovers another dog holding what looks like a similar bone.

The dog decides that he must have that other bone as well. He then opens his mouth and attempts to grasp the "other" bone in the other dog's mouth. To his own chagrin, the clever mutt loses his own bone and gains nothing. This begs the question;

"What does it profit a man to gain the whole world, and lose his own soul?"

This chapter examines biblical characters such as "The Rich Young Ruler", "The Rich Fool", "The Rich Man and Lazarus", King Ahab, King Solomon, and others. It compares and contrasts the biblical characters and uses them to show the futility of attempting to gain wealth by "growing rich". It also examines modern "rich" persons (in the public domain) such as lottery winners, movie stars, musical stars, scam artists, and sports stars, many of whom became rich overnight (whose names will be changed to protect their identities), but eventually squandered their endowments due to carelessness and arrogance.

The State of Being Rich

This state is one often desired by many who follow the world's capitalist, free market oriented system. For many, being "rich" conjures up ideas of limitless access to money and resources. Being "rich" actually has lots of different definitions depending on where you live in the world, and with whom you are categorizing yourself. Being rich has to do with an individual's desired lifestyle, along with their individual wants.

Back in 2009, he was driving along with his nephew, who was probably twelve (12) years old at the time, through what looked like a chique suburban neighborhood of Southern Florida. His nephew Byron then remarked, “Uncle Keith, these are such nice houses around here. All of these people must be rich??!”

The young nephew was quite surprised at his uncle’s response to the question. Based on Keith's knowledge of the district they were driving through, he said, "I am sure many of them desire to be so, but most of them may still owe lots of money on their mortgages in these nice homes. If they do not pay, they will eventually be asked to leave them. That is not a state that people really want to be in at all, despite how nice their homes look on the outside."

This is the problem of being perceived as "rich". It is based on external perception and not reality in many instances.

According to The Wall Street Journal (www.wsj.com/articles), Samuel Johnson once made this statement;

"Every man is rich or poor according to the proportion between his desires and his enjoyment."

What Johnson is suggesting is that perceived "richness" (note: not wealth) or "poorness" is based on the place in that person's mind where he/she wants to be comfortable physically and emotionally. This will inevitably translate to different levels of required income and resources to attain the desired state of being. In other words, the larger the gap between your desired lifestyle and what you are able to enjoy now, based on Johnson's explanation, is how "rich" a person is in his and the view of others.

This is the problem of defining what it means to be "rich". It's the reason why many who are pursuing riches in life become fickle and vain in their attempts to attain this state of being.

As a result of the above, many high net worth individuals (defined as having investable assets in excess of one million United States Dollars or more) and rubber high net worth individuals are never satisfied with their level income, and access to resources, despite many "rich" people being in the top one percent (1%) of the top tier income bracket worldwide.

Those who are or want to be "rich" as a state of being, are never satisfied with their present state of affairs. Some will say that not being satisfied is a good thing, as the individual has an incentive to achieve more.

The question is, for what purpose are the "rich" accumulating and hoarding "things"? Is it just to feel better about their low self-esteem in relation to others? If this is the motive for growing rich, then this will leave one always in a state of wanting and feeling of lack when compared to others.

The State of Being Wealthy

The word wealth for purposes of this book will be viewed as ALL assets of an individual whether physical assets (houses, lands, cars, art, precious metals, furniture, etc.), monetary assets (cash, monetary instruments, stock, bonds, commodity notes etc), along with other critical assets such as spiritual wellbeing, emotional wellbeing, intellectual capital, social capital, and physical health.

This broad definition of wealth not only encompasses possessions, social and lifestyle based definitions (which people tended to base "being rich" upon). We will see that being wealthy provides a much more wholesome lifestyle than those who class themselves as rich.

The wealthy individual may have lots of possessions, but he /she does not define himself by those things he owns. The wealthy person is not caught up in the illusion of who his or her neighbors are, and how well monetarily those neighbors are doing.

The wealthy individual is not worried over market oriented conditions, for his faith is not subject to conditions on Wall Street or at The London Stock Exchange. The wealthy may be marginally affected by the ups and downs of the free market system, but he understands that (as the biblical Billionaire of his day Job, when faced with a free market crash and subsequent Great Depression personally).

"The Lord giveth and The Lord taketh away, blessed be the name of Yahweh". (Zondervan King James Version Study Bible, Job Chapter 2:21)

The wealthy recognize that free market forces are controlled by the rulers of this world's economy through decision-making (i.e. taxes, war, fiscal policy), natural forces of nature that affect climate, weather conditions, as well as human nature (crime, terrorism, market scams etc). Faith based individuals understand that all such things are ultimately SUBJECT to control by GOD (HEAVENLY FATHER YAHWEH), and his will.

The wealthy are not afraid of risks inherent in the free market, but exercise wisdom and forethought in making decisions about investing and asset management. They do not make sudden and drastic lifestyle changes to accommodate new found wealth. A good example of this is Billionaire Warren Buffet who has remained in the same modest house, in a typical middle class neighborhood for decades in the mid-western United States, despite being one of the world's wealthiest Billionaires. Buffet understood early on that the trimmings of wealth are of far less importance than retaining your personal values. This is a true characteristic of a wealthy man.

CHAPTER FOUR: EGYPT: THE WORLD'S FIRST WEALTHY SUPERPOWER

The Chapter "Egypt: The Ancient World's Superpower", examines the origins of Western civilization. Ancient Egypt during the time of The Pharaohs is examined. The biblical characters of Vizier Joseph, and Prince Moses are examined. These are key individuals who became the beneficiaries of the first and second Egyptian Wealth transfers in particular. The Ancient Egyptian economy is looked at to examine Egypt's source of wealth.

It must be keenly noted that Egypt brought us the source of a great proportion of modern financial wealth today, the papyrus or "paper". Modern street lingo phrases such as "gotta make this paper", and "trying to get a million dead Presidents" all have their root origins in the Egyptian invention of paper.

Egypt is recognized as the cradle of Western civilization for more than one reason. If one looks closely at the U.S. dollar, one will see a familiar Egyptian innovation. It's called the pyramid.

Encapsulated in this pyramid on the dollar note, is the "all seeing eye", which some suggest represents God's (Yahweh's) eye.

We do not know if this image gives credit to ancient Egypt for America's assent to world domination, but we do know that Egypt's contributions to ancient civilization form much of the foundation for which we in modern Western civilization enjoy today.

The first stone buildings erected by man (The Pyramids) were built by The Egyptians (Collier's Encyclopedia, Volume eight – 8, page 658). Long before Aristotle, and Plato (Greek Philosophers), The Egyptian pyramid architect and Mathematician Imhotep (pronounced Him-O-tep) is recognized as the first genius of the ancient world (Collier's page 658).

The Egyptians devised a calendar, along with what is now, "the calendar year". This really allowed man to document times and seasons. The year, derived from an agricultural term, allowed the eventual development of "the fiscal year", as well as the accounting "financial year". Documenting time is critical to modern accounting and payment cycles.

The Egyptians were the second civilization to develop an advanced code of writing. This system of writing became known as hieroglyphics. So advanced was this code of written language that it was not until the 1700's, that one of French Emperor Napoleon's Soldiers accidentally discovered the famous "Rosetta Stone". This allowed the ancient language to be deciphered in modern times for the first time.

However, Egypt's greatest contributions to Western civilization came in the form of its art, architecture, and elaborate structure of bureaucracy and public administration.

The great kings of Asia during ancient times held the belief that the precious metal called gold, was as common as dust in the desert regions of Egypt (Colliers page 673).

The Nile River gave Egypt its agricultural wealth, which continued well into the advent of The Roman Empire. Egypt was in fact the bread basket of The Roman Empire, and was known as an ally, protectorate state of Rome, never being occupied as a Roman Province.

The wealth of Egypt if quantified in today's dollars, at any point of the old and new dynastic periods probably equated to several hundreds of billions of today's U.S. dollars in any one standard calendar year. Keith Seele (Collier's Page 671) in speaking about the economy and wealth of ancient Egypt noted;

"...the yields of the fields in grain and in domestic livestock were handled in incalculable amounts (by even today's standards)."

A key determinant of the wealth of any civilization must be seen in terms of its architectural achievements, it's fine art and sculpture, advanced culture, religious tradition, access to seemingly incalculable monetary based possessions, orderly social structure, administrative bureaucracy and systems, economic structure, and of course in the strength of its merchant shipping (for imports), its armies and navy.

Monetary possessions are only one determinant factor of the wealth of a nation. Egypt's wealth has long been sought after by great nations, including France, Britain, Germany, and indeed, The United States, which all have museums and University Departments specifically designated to display Ancient Egyptian wealth. Ancient Egypt is in fact the only civilization that has a branch of science purely dedicated to discovering its wealth, called Egyptology.

There is no "Greektology", "Mesopatamiology", “Chinatology", "Babyloniatology", or "Rheumatology" for instance. This in and out itself speaks to the immense Wealth of Egypt.

What does all of this wealth have to do with you? If you are a Believer in The Heavenly Father, and follow the Judeo Christian faith, then understanding The Wealth of Egypt has major implications on the level of your own personal wealth or lack thereof in today's twenty first (21st) century free market economy.

CHAPTER FIVE: WHY WEALTH TRANSFERS ARE IMPORTANT

Wealth transfers occur every day in a free market, capitalist society like ours. Every minute of every hour, someone or some group has either granted someone else a wealth transfer or has been the recipient of a wealth transfer.

Wealth transfers are important because they move wealth to the more productive members of society, to advance the society.

Some wealth transfers are automatic and occur not by the hand of a man, but by the programmed sequences of a computer system. Some wealth transfers are perfectly legal. Others are more dubious.

Some occur by a government agency. Most emanate from private firms, agencies, and individuals.

You have been both the benefactor and the beneficiary of wealth transfers in the past. If you are a part of the Judeo Christian tradition, you are periodically called upon to transfer ten percent (10) % of your increased wealth to your church, synagogue, or house of worship.

At Christmas time, if you have ever stopped by a red pot, with someone ringing a handbell, and have made a dollar donation, you have just made a wealth transfer.

If you are an immigrant and you have gone to a Western Union office to send some money to a foreign relative as a gift, you have made a type of wealth transfer called a remittance. For some third (3rd) world countries, remittances represent an entire sector of the national economy!

A wealth transfer is any activity involving the movement of valuable assets from the ownership of one person or entity, to another person or entity. Governments do it, private companies do it, nonprofit organizations do it, rich people do it, poor people do it, small businesses do it, large businesses do it, and definitely wealthy people do it.

A wealth transfer can be obligatory or non-obligatory. It can have contractual conditions, or be non-contractual in nature. It can be performance or nonperformance based. It can be conditional or unconditional.

Physical assets or intangible assets may be involved.

Obtaining a raise on a job is not a wealth transfer. What you are doing is exchanging an even more valuable asset called TIME for monetary compensation, which in many instances is not commensurate with the value of the asset which you are offering for exchange. Time is our most valuable resource.

Jobs are very important. Someone has to do the work. Someone has to get up and "make the donuts", as in the classic 1980's commercial by Dunkin Donuts. Somebody has to stand guard to protect the bank from armed bandits trying to illegally obtain the bank's assets. Someone has to fly the airplane or deliver the mail.

Someone has to help others file their taxes, or give them options for investing their wealth.

Someone has to help build or repair the millions of miles of roadways in North America so that the rest of us can drive on them to get to our destinations. Someone has to be on the other end of the call center line to answer questions related to setting up the new smart HD television we just bought. Here is the breakthrough moment in your life:

"IT DOES NOT HAVE TO BE YOU!" 24

Or even if it is you for a time, it does not have to be you for your entire life.

There is nothing wrong with work. We all have to work in some way shape or form. But; when we as Believers can use our power to obtain wealth, we can decide in what form that work comes; for what periods we will work or not work; for whom we will work; and what activities we will do when we work. That is the power of wealth. It gives us God's most valuable gift; the power of choice.

When we have wealth we can, under The Heavenly Father's direction, help to chart our own destiny, and have more time to carry out his will for our lives.

Seizing wealth transfers, and having the wisdom, knowledge and understanding to properly manage the wealth once received, not only benefits our own lives but the lives of those around us. Wealth can be used to glorify God (Yahweh) in our own lives towards others, who having seen us struggle for years, can gain hope that our heavenly Father will never leave us nor forsake us, despite our troubles. Sharing our testimony following the obtaining of wealth can help other Believers obtain theirs as well.

Only those who grow rich, however, do not wish to share their secrets to abundance, and eventually hoard all things associated with their richness. Wealth transfers show that God (Yahweh) is faithful to his covenant to our fathers (Abraham, Isaac, and Jacob), and that his promises to his people are Yay and Amen. This chapter will examine fifteen types of wealth transfers, most of which we have the power to obtain through faith and perseverance.

CHAPTER SIX: FROM VICTIMIZED TO VILLAN TO VIZIER THE FIRST GREAT EGYPTIAN WEALTH TRANSFER TO JOSEPH

On a starry wilderness night, a young seventeen year old shepherd boy after securing his flock of sheep, laid down to sleep, probably exhausted from his work of the day.

This was no ordinary night, however. The Shepherd boy drifted off into REM sleep, where dreams are made. He then saw a peculiar sight. He saw himself in a great bountiful field, binding sheaves of grain together. Then his eleven brothers appeared suddenly, also binding their sheaves of grain for harvesting.

Following this, the young shepherd saw something amazing. Suddenly his sheaves stood upright and tall. Immediately his brothers harvested sheaves of grain, bowed, and paid homage to their brother's sheaves. He had to tell his brothers what he saw the next day. But expecting them to be happy, he met cold, hard looks from his brothers who immediately knew the interpretation of the dream without prompting and said;

"So!!! You are going to be a ruler over us!!"

(Zondervan King James Version, Genesis 37: 5-11 Page 79).

Joseph was the son of a wealthy herdsman and trader named Jacob. Of Joseph's father, it is written;

"And Jacob dwelt in the land wherewith his father was a stranger, in the land of Canaan." Jacob who in his youth could be defined as a "trickster" or "scam artist" had obtained the favor of God (Yahweh) nonetheless and was to inherit the land of Canaan, to fulfill God's promise to Abraham that;

"I will make of thee a great nation, and I will bless thee, and make thy name great, and thou shall be a blessing:"

(Genesis 12, Verse 2, Zondervan KJV, Page 29).

Our heavenly Father wants all believers in his name to be a blessing to their family, their neighborhoods, their communities, their region, state, and country. This is the key reason for wealth transfers.

So how does a promise of blessings to the patriarch Abraham, connect with a seventeen (17) year old boy having a dream in a field?

It has everything to do with it.

Joseph was to be the conduit through which the transformation of a band of sheep herders into a wealthy nation, would occur. For a nation to be formed, a transfer of wealth is essential.

So the "dreamer", a seventeen (17) year old shepherd boy, was to later endure hardships on his brothers' behalf. These hardships included being left for dead in a pit. Being sold into slavery in the land of Egypt. Being accused of a crime he did not commit, and then thrown into prison on 'trumped up charges" as a result. He would then while in prison, help to restore a royal aide back to his office, and then be forgotten about by the same ungrateful aide. And then, one day the shepherd boy would be rushed to get a shave, and haircut to meet the Ruler of a great world power, Pharaoh, The King of Egypt, who had a big PROBLEM no one could solve around him.

Hold onto your dreams. Do let anyone discourage you from dreaming.

Joseph would give Pharaoh, "The thing" which solved his problem. That "thing", demanded an immediate wealth transfer to be at least partly compensated.

How much would The United States have paid to stop The Great Depression of the 1930s?

Or how much would the captains of industry would have paid to advertise the 2008 economic meltdown, the worst since 1933?

It would have been priceless. If someone could have gone to Congress and the White House, and given them a blueprint in 2007, which would have softened the ensuing economic disaster of 2008 how, might that person have been rewarded? Perhaps in the millions? Tens of millions?

Hundreds of millions? Billions?

The reward would certainly have been commensurate with the problem that was being solved.

When an unsolvable problem emerges, a wealth transfer must occur in favor of the one who provides a practical working solution.

That is the magnitude of what Joseph (under God's inspiration) achieved in Egypt. He solved a problem that all of Pharaoh's hoard of advisers, scientists, learned men, economists, religious gurus, specialists, and experts could not.

Every company, organization, community, city, municipality, federal government agency, and economy has problems, which need to be solved now. Problems exist all around us. This is the key to initiating your wealth transfer. FIND A PROBLEM and SOLVE IT.

So, Joseph's talent in dream interpretation made him a "Dreamologist"!! Joseph's unique talent and services which were felt to be of no value by his family, his former boss (Potiphar), and the initially ungrateful Egyptian Royal Aide to Pharaoh (The Cup Bearer), would now pay unbelievable, unfathomable, and unthinkable dividends for Joseph. His services and talents were now in high demand by the economy of The Kingdom of Egypt.

Joseph had given Pharaoh, The King of Egypt the "thing" that would save the Egyptian economy and civilization.

What "thing" do you have that can save your community?

There is some "thing" in all Believers which can unleash their God destined wealth transfer.

Superpowers are made once every thousand years. Joseph, because of the demand placed on his talent and training, would move Egypt from a mere economic and military power in the known world at that time, to become the first superpower.

Joseph whose talent in dream interpretation, coupled with his understanding of management, administration, finance and economics, would actually propel him to the office of Vizier and Secretary of The Treasury in today's terms. Here is what the bible says of Joseph's confirmation ceremony;

"And the thing was good in the eyes of Pharaoh and in the eyes of all his servants. (or modern-day cabinet)".

(Genesis 41:42, Zondervan KJV, page 87).

The 'thing" is the management and economic plan that Joseph outlines to Pharaoh for advertising a crisis and certain disaster to the Egyptian economy.

So now, Joseph is about to become the recipient along with his family, the tribes of Israel, of the first major wealth transfer from Egypt.

"See, I set thee over all the land of Egypt." (Zondervan KJV, page 87).

And now here comes the actual symbolic wealth transfer to Joseph and the tribes of Israel;

"And Pharaoh took off his ring from his hand, and put it upon Joseph's hand, and arrayed him in vestures of fine linen, and put a gold chain about his neck."

With The King of Egypt performing this gesture, he has in turn transferred "trusteeship" and stewardship of Egypt's vast wealth into the hands of a former sheep herder from the plains of Canaan.

The Egyptian economy at this time would have been valued in the hundreds of billions if we calculated according to today's valuations of the known treasures of Egypt.

Ancient Egypt's vast wealth was vested in its administrative bureaucracy for the most part (of which now Joseph was ruler on behalf of The Pharaoh). So thus we can conclude that Joseph was made a high net worth individual (with investable assets in excess of ten million dollars overnight) in Egypt.

The wealth transfer continued throughout the life of Joseph and would later be extended to the tribes of Israel.

"Now when Jacob saw that there was corn in Egypt, Jacob said unto his sons, Why do ye look upon one another?" (Zondervan KJV page 89).

The Patriarch goes on:

"Behold, I have heard that there is corn in Egypt: get you down thither, and buy for us, from thence; that we may live, and not die."

(Zondervan KJV, page 89).

The actual wealth transfer would follow when Jacob and Joseph's brothers would migrate from Canaan to sojourn in Egypt. Upon meeting Pharaoh, here is what transpires:

"And Pharaoh spoke unto Joseph...The land of Egypt is before thee; in the best of the land make thy father and brethren dwell."

So we see that the Tribes of Israel also become rulers in Egypt and the co beneficiaries of the first great wealth transfer from Egypt.

The wealth transfer from Egypt continues:

"And Joseph placed his father and his brethren, and gave them a POSSESSION in the land of Egypt, in the best of the land....as Pharaoh (King of Egypt) had commanded."

But here is the fascinating twist that occurred following Pharaoh's bequeath to the tribes. The Bible goes on to say:

"And Jacob blessed Pharaoh"

Wealth follows blessing. Jacob actually brought something more valuable than Pharaoh's wealth. For him, he carried the blessings of Abraham. Even though Joseph gave Pharaoh 'The thing' that would save Egypt, the cradle of Western civilization; God (Yahweh) allowed his father Jacob to bless Egypt in an even greater way.

As Believers, we carry a great blessing with us that the world may not recognize, but which it demands and needs. This is why we have the power to obtain wealth, for we carry 'the blessing' with us.

God seems to love sheep herders, or people of lowly estates to become the recipients of wealth transfers. So we as Believers are eligible. Jacob was a keeper of livestock/sheep, David was a lowly shepherd boy, and Joseph was also a shepherd boy.

Do not believe that Pharaoh was this "nice guy" who loved giving away money to people in need. Pharaoh was still a worshipper of idols and false gods. Egypt in fact regarded Pharaoh himself as a god king. Pharaoh was a shrewd businessman, who recognized that he stood on the threshold of losing everything, and being less competitive than his neighbors if he did not follow Joseph's wise counsel.

When faced with impending disaster, Pharaoh humbled himself before God (Yahweh's) servant Joseph and recognized that Joseph was able to solve an impossible problem for which no one else could. Joseph's gender, ethnicity (being Hebrew), race, nationality, marital status, education level, poverty, and looks, became irrelevant. These are things some believers use as barriers to their self-image. Joseph's innate talents placed a wealth transfer demand on the economic resources of Egypt in his favor, and not only his favor, but that of ALL those who were even loosely affiliated with him!! That's the power of wealth.

Shrewd business people are not so much concerned with empowering others, through wealth transfers as they are in preserving and growing their own wealth. The price they pay is irrelevant to the objective of preserving and growing their assets.

People of great means lack something that the true believer has. The blessing of Abraham. You see, Joseph had more power than the entire economy and political structure of Egypt. He had a solution to a problem. Being rich, without solutions to problems, is like a ship with oil and gold, with no port of destination to offload and trade.

What "thing" do you have that can solve a problem for others? What's your "thing"?

Is it your baking skills thing? Your mechanical skills thing? Your business skills thing? Your management skills thing? Your artistic skills thing? Your home decorating skills thing? Your cake decorating skills thing? Your cycling skills? Your writing skills? Your dancing skills? Your singing skills? Your planning skills?

That God (Yahweh) given "thing" is the key to beginning the process of a wealth transfer to you. We will look further at these things in Chapter Nine (9).

CHAPTER SEVEN: THE SECOND GREAT EGYPTIAN WEALTH TRANSFER: MOSES, PRINCE OF EGYPT

Joseph is now Vizier of Egypt, second in command only to Pharaoh, The King. Following the seven years of plenty, Joseph's system has to now prove that it is able to save Egypt from destruction in face of a worldwide famine or great depression.

The economy of Egypt is still brought to its knees despite Joseph's management system being in place. Other lands however were wiped out, including Canaan, which had no system of reserves. The Bible records:

"All the land of Egypt and Canaan fainted because of the famine." (Genesis Chapter 47, verse 12, Zondervan KJV page 98).

But Egypt, because of Joseph's solution, does not ultimately crumble. The financial system of Egypt collapses. Anyway, however:

"And when money failed in the land of Egypt, and in the land of Canaan, all the Egyptians came unto Joseph and said, Give us bread for why should we die in thy presence? For the money faileth."

Here is a very important difference between those who are merely rich, and those who are wealthy. There have been times in the global economy when money became worthless, and possessions also became literally worthless. When this happens, rich people, who have not created a wealth producing system will perish.

A wealth producing system is some "thing", that can outlast both good times and famine.

There were two times in recent history when paper money literally became worthless. In the 1920s, hyperinflation consumed nations like Germany, where it literally took a wheelbarrow of Deutschmarks to buy a loaf of bread. The German financial system collapsed under The Weimar Republic. Holding money as a source of wealth was worthless in

Germany and other European countries.

The next time in recent memory where money 'failed' was following the great Wall Street crash of 1929 in The United States. Persons who had money in the banks, lost most if not all of it overnight, for there were runs on the majority of U.S. banks at that time. Banks literally could not pay their depositors the value of their cash deposits.

Many rich people went into abject poverty overnight. Their money held in banks was worthless. Stocks and shares held in banks were also worthless. Many committed suicide after losing everything they owned.

Do you know that if you have a million dollars in the bank, if there is a run on a bank, you are only insured with The Federal Deposit Insurance Corporation (FDIC) for up to two hundred and fifty thousand dollars? This really means that in the event of an unforeseen disaster, your money held in banks is automatically only worth a quarter of its face value above two hundred and fifty thousand dollars ($250,000.00). This will also have an impact on depositors with less than two hundred and fifty thousand dollars ($250,000) as well.

Rising Federal government deficits can also eventually have an impact on the value of The U.S. dollar in the future, as some global investors may begin shifting investments from U.S. Dollar based ones if rising Federal budgetary deficits persist into the future.

In 2008 many also lost homes, investments, and business interests as a result of the mortgage bubble bursting. To tackle the situation, consecutive U.S governments (The Bush and Obama Administrations) had to institute (with the authorization of Congress) massive government bailout plans in the trillions of dollars to stop the complete collapse of the American and global economies.

This is one reason why God (Yahweh) does not urge his people to "place their trust in riches". The wealthy place their trust in God (Yahweh), not riches.

Moving on, the bible records, that four hundred (400) years after Joseph leaves the scene, only his bones are left:

"And the children of Israel were fruitful, and increased abundantly, and multiplied, and waxed exceeding mighty, and the land was filled with them." (Exodus 1:1, Zondervan KJV, page112).

This is the ultimate fulfillment of the first Egyptian wealth transfer. The tribes of Israel are now growing into a nation and prospering in the Egyptian Kingdom. This is where friction and problems now occur. It is recorded:

"Now there arose a new King over Egypt, who knew not Joseph." (Exodus 1:8, Zondervan KJV, page 112).

This king made an edict (a law) enslaving the children of Israel saying: "Behold, the people of the children of Israel are more and mightier than we" (Exodus 1:9, Zondervan KJV, page 112).

This in itself speaks to the power of the wealth transfer from Egypt four hundred (400) years earlier. Generations of Israelite tribesmen became wealthy after Joseph and his brothers had died.

That is the power of true wealth. The wealthy leave a legacy and a system of wealth accumulation for the generations to come.

Enter Moses, a child born into slavery. He was in fact not even supposed to live, for Pharaoh King of Egypt had ordered all male born children born to Hebrews to be killed by the midwives. Moses' mother in desperation threw Moses into the River Nile hoping to avoid the death of her son. It worked.

It just so happened that The Pharaoh's daughter went with her handmaidens to bathe in the river at about the same time as Moses was placed in a basket to drift amongst the reeds.

The raft caught the attention of Pharaoh's daughter, who ordered her handmaids to grab it.

Upon seeing the contents being held within the basket, The Princess was moved with compassion. She immediately adopted the boy child as her own. The boy would receive a nanny, who, as circumstances permitted, would end up being his own Israelite mother.

And so we now have a Hebrew boy, who grew up in Pharaoh's palace as his own grandson, a prince of Egypt. As Prince of Egypt, Moses grew up in a life of privilege. He would be educated in the language, customs, and sciences of Egypt. As a prince, he would learn about the Egyptian systems of bureaucracy and the art of war. The young Egyptian prince would be treated as royalty, and would eventually become involved in Pharaoh's massive building projects. Going to check on the Children of Israel in bondage from time to time.

Of course, Moses would learn key qualities of leadership as a Prince. All of this unknown to him, would be valuable preparation for eventually becoming the leader of his own nation of Israel.

During these years, Moses was developing his intellectual capital, a key component of managing wealth. Intellectual capital refers to those assets of the mind. Those assets are related to how to manage and plan for wealth. It (intellectual capital) relates to making sound business decisions, and recognizing valuable opportunities, and potential risks and threats. But most importantly, intellectual capital relates to the ability to think creatively and think outside of the box, to solve problems. Intellectual capital is God's (Yahweh's) investment in the minds of the wealthy.

Becoming rich, without investing in developing the mind is a recipe for problems. How tough does one invest in the mind?

One builds intellectual capital not necessarily by attending an institution of higher learning, though this may make a contribution to building intellectual capital. The curriculum of Universities and Colleges do not teach how an individual can become wealthy. Most business classes teach concepts related to how to help manage someone else's wealth or richness in most instances. How to grow someone else's investment portfolio and/or manage someone else's company.

Where universities do teach Entrepreneurship, it is from a very theoretical perspective. True entrepreneurs endow themselves with intellectual capital from varied sources. These sources include reading stories about successful business people, watching documentaries on successful entrepreneurs, being involved in some level of business themselves, as well as taking on a mentor.

So we see that Moses grew up as a Royal Prince, and was in fact mentored by the leader of a superpower nation, in preparation for leading his own loose band of tribes, destined to become a great nation.

Moses' temper, however, would become a thorn in his side and would cause him to flee Egypt for some forty (40) years. Following the burning bush experience, where God (Yahweh) orders him back to Egypt to deliver The children of Israel, he would return to Egypt to oversee one of the greatest wealth transfers in history.

This wealth transfer would essentially last even into the present twenty first (21st) century. Israelis today are amongst the wealthiest in the world, in some instances controlling entire industries, including global finance, media, and several others. Amongst famous and wealthy Hebrew families spanning generations, are The Rothschilds for instance, who control a gigantic global financial wealth building system.

At the burning bush, God (Yahweh) tells Moses exactly how the wealth transfer will occur. Here's what he says:

"And I will give these people favor in the sight of the Egyptians, and it shall Come to pass that when ye go, ye shall not go empty:" (Exodus 3:21, Zondervan KJV, page 116).

And now God (Yahweh) speaks of the second great Egyptian wealth transfer to the nation of Israel:

"But every woman shall borrow from her neighbor and her that. Sojourneth in her house, jewels of silver, and jewels of gold, and raiment: And ye shall put them upon your sons and upon your daughters." (Exodus 3: 22, Zondervan KJV, page 116).

And the wealth transfer is now to be established by God (Yahweh) himself, as evidenced here when he says;

"And ye shall spoil the Egyptians" (Exodus 3:22, Zondervan KJV, page 117).

Barker et al (Zondervan KJV, page 116), indicate that the spoil of which God (Yahweh) speaks is connected directly to God's (Yahweh's) promise to Abraham, that though Israel would be enslaved for four hundred – 400 years, they would leave with great substance; in other words they would leave very wealthy.

This wealth also included the intellectual capital gained from the Egypt experience. It would eventually contribute to Israel itself becoming a superpower nation under King Solomon.

CHAPTER EIGHT: MODERN GREAT WEALTH TRANSFERS

Wealth transfers are by no means a thing of a distant past. Wealth transfers occur on a daily basis. Most of us are totally unaware of the wealth transfers taking place all around us every day.

There is however a system to tap into wealth transfers. We will begin by looking at more general nation to nation wealth transfers first.

In 1946, one of the largest wealth transfers occurred between nations in the form of the Marshall Plan. The United States and The Allies (including Britain, France, Canada, and Australia, etc) had just defeated the Axis powers (Germany, Italy, Japan, Romania, Turkey, etc.) in World War Two (2).

Europe was completely devastated as a result of the bloodiest war in human history. The United States would emerge as the world's first superpower nation of the twentieth (20th) century.

The Marshall Plan transferred hundreds of billions of dollars to devastated European countries including West Germany. Europe had to be rebuilt. The Marshall Plan transferred massive amounts of wealth to European citizens. Within ten (10) years after World War 2, Europe was rebuilt and began to emerge as a collective power in the world once again.

The growth of super global companies such as Airbus Industries and Volkswagen were the direct result of this transfer, following the creation of The European Economic Community (EEC), followed by The European Union (EU).

This wealth transfer was initiated by The U.S. Federal Government at the time.

The next great United States wealth transfer took place more slowly, and calculating, and was initiated by Corporate America rather than the Federal government itself.

This would have begun with the travel of United States President Richard Nixon, in 1972 to China. This move by Nixon softened US-Sino relations and marked the beginning of a new era of trade between The U.S. and China. This trade would not truly blossom until the twenty first century, when U.S. companies began moving large chunks of their manufacturing operations to Chinese cities.

This wealth transfer virtually brought small town America to a grinding halt. The phenomenon was known as "Outsourcing". Manufacturing hubs in American states such as Ohio, Pennsylvania, and other states felt the brunt of this transfer of wealth overseas to China, by rich special interest corporate America.

The Captains of manufacturing industries had lost faith in America's ability to manufacture goods competitively. As a result, they orchestrated one of the greatest national wealth transfers in history, sending millions of jobs overseas.

This wealth transfer made thousands of new Chinese Multi-millionaires overnight. The rich owners of manufacturing plants were prepared to sacrifice quality for increased profits. As a result what these leaders did was make The United States less affluent economically in the world, while growing the economy of China.

As a result, China became even more competitive in relation to American manufacturing, which compounded the problem. These "rich" industrialists were not prepared to find innovative means of making American industry more competitive by obtaining more intellectual capital (in the form of increased research and development budgets and innovative solutions). The country which through its manufacturing industries won World War two (2), and allowed it to become a superpower, no longer had the drive to innovate, and instead, gave a massive wealth transfer to The People's Republic of China, over a period of years, to "save a few bucks."

U.S. companies are now beginning to realize that it is becoming more expensive nowadays to do business in China, in the face of lessening available commercial space in manufacturing centers like Shanghai, along with Chinese worker agitation for increased wages. There is now what appears to be the beginnings of a growing "flight of capital" to destinations outside of China, by many Chinese Multimillionaires. Also, China is now hitting its quotas for imports into The U.S.A., which has a serious impact on its ability to expand in U.S. markets. This however has not stopped considerably the massive growth of The Chinese economy.

Many U.S. companies are now looking inward again for solutions to making their products more competitive. They are seeking solutions in the form of new product idea submissions domestically. They are seeking solutions to productivity issues, management effectiveness, and employee efficiency. This represents a tremendous opportunity for your own wealth transfer.

CHAPTER NINE: HOW TO OBTAIN YOUR WEALTH TRANSFER

Moses led the children of Israel out of captivity and into The Sinai desert, after four hundred

(400) years of bondage. When the children of Israel had departed out of the land of Egypt, they "spoiled The Egyptians", and took a great proportion of wealth into the wilderness.

After overcoming the tremendous sorrow of losing his firstborn son, and heir to his throne, The Egyptian Pharaoh suddenly realized that a substantial amount of wealth had been extracted from Egypt by The Israelites.

Furious, Pharaoh orders his royal guards to saddle up and go behind Israel to recapture the tremendous wealth that had been transferred with their departure. The new nation of Israel would soon find itself between a rock and a hard place.

As Pharaoh and his soldiers pursued them, the band of tribes approached The Red Sea. They faced a daunting prospect. Returning to slavery in Egypt or dying in the wilderness at the hands of Pharaoh's army. They (The Children of Israel) then place an enormous amount of pressure on Moses, by making this sarcastic statement:

"Because there were no graves in Egypt, hast thou taken us away to die in the wilderness?" (Exodus 14:11, Zondervan KJV, page 136).

There must be something in mind at this point. Wealthy people are leaders, who many times face criticism, from the very people they are called to empower.

The responsibilities of being wealthy are sometimes more than most people can take. Most people prefer to remain in bondage to their inadequate jobs, careers, and way of life.

Becoming a wealthy individual demands great sacrifice and fortitude. It demands your time, and energy, in whatever path you will take to achieve your wealth transfer. Daily, you have to be committed to staying the course to placing a demand on the economic system, to release your wealth.

Sometimes, those closest to you do not understand the steps that have to be taken to achieve your wealth transfer and will attempt to discourage you, as the children of Israel tried to do to Moses:

"Is not this the word that we did tell thee in Egypt, saying, let us alone, that we may serve the Egyptians? For it had been better for us to serve the Egyptians, than that we should die in the wilderness."

The children of Israel at this point forgot everything that The Heavenly Father had done for them. They were displaying a total lack of faith in their newly found freedom from bondage.

Becoming a wealthy person requires faith. Without faith, it is virtually impossible to use the power The Heavenly Father has given you to obtain wealth. It takes faith to not short circuit the process, and to borrow from a military expression, to 'stay on mission".

The previous wealth transfers from Egypt, which were ultimately orchestrated by The Heavenly Father, were not to be compared to the ultimate transfer that was coming for these people; the promise of the conquest of a land so wealthy that it "flowed with milk and honey".

But now the wealth transfer for the Israelites was becoming too burdensome. This brings us to a very serious point here.

WEALTH TRANSFERS ARE NOT FOR EVERYBODY

Many may desire the freedom that wealth affords. Many desire the trimmings of wealth (the side effects of affluence exotic vacation homes, exotic cars, and financial independence), but are not prepared to handle the responsibilities of wealth when it arrives.

So now, Moses and the children of Israel are between a rock and a hard place. Moses himself begins to doubt the power of the Heavenly Father and cries out asking for help. The words of The Father come back to him from the burning bush experience.

At the burning bush, when Moses learns of God's (Yahweh's) plan to deliver the children of Israel from their bondage, Moses makes this comment of doubt:

"But behold, they will not believe me, nor hearken unto my voice: for they will say.

The Lord hath not sent thee." (Exodus 4:1, Zondervan KJV, page 32).

Moses was genuinely concerned about the people's response to his claim that God (Yahweh) would deliver them. He knew that four hundred (400) years of slavery would impact the psyche of a people suffering under bondage. These were people who experienced generations of slavery and subservience to a great and powerful nation. It would not be easy for these people to emancipate from the mental conditions imposed on them by slavery.

Poverty itself is a form of mental slavery. It conditions people to think in a certain way. Circumstances force families to socialize their young for survival and self-preservation at all costs. Decision making is therefore primarily concerned with survival, rather than taking an introspective look at their full God (Yahweh) given potential.

The state of being "rich" is also a type of intellectual bondage. The obsession of the rich is how not to become poor or poor again. This type of mentality not only closes itself up from becoming a "giving personality", but is also only concerned with self-preservation.

These are the problems of being rich and poor. The poor are obsessed with issues of daily survival. The rich are concerned with issues of self-preservation (which really is a higher level of survival). Many of both the poor and the rich miss valuable opportunities for genuine happiness and peace in this life. There are exceptions of course.

The poor man who accepts Christ (Yahshua) will find contentment but still has a responsibility to find and "turn over" his/her talents (as seen in The Parable of The Talents).

The rich man (as in the biblical story of The Tax Collector Zacheus), can repent of his ways of selfishness (being obsessed with self-preservation) and experience a new life by transitioning from rich to wealthy.

The problem many of the rich face however the daunting task of breaking their identity and self-image is. This can be seen in the biblical story of the rich young ruler. As a result of sticking to the mentality of being rich, which he inherited, the rich young ruler could not possess the true wealth Jesus (Yahshua) wanted to transfer to him.

As a result, Jesus gave his famous words about those who define themselves as rich:

"It is easier for the camel to pass through the eye of a needle, then for a rich man to enter the kingdom of heaven." (Matthew 19: 24, Zondervan KJV, page 1,974). So back to Moses at the burning bush.

God (Yahweh's) response to Moses' doubt was in the form of a simple question.

What Is In Thine Hand

The key to affecting your own wealth transfer lies in this simple question God (Yahweh) poses to Moses.

What Moses had in his hand was a simple shepherd's rod. This rod would be used to initiate the second great wealth transfer from Egypt, but would also maintain the wealth transfer when Moses uses it as an instrument of faith to part the Red Sea.

What is needed to affect your personal wealth transfer is already "in your hand". It comes in the form of your skills, experience, knowledge, and character.

Most of us remain in debt, poverty, and trying to make ends meet because we do not know what is in our hands. We are either unfamiliar with or do not know the extent of the "power" we really have to obtain wealth. We have never taken an introspective examination of ourselves and the treasure of what God (Yahweh) has given us.

If you are a Believer in Christ (Yahshua), and follow God (Yahweh's) basic statutes, you are already wired for wealth.

You already have the characteristics and traits of wealthy people. You would be a natural giver, expecting nothing in return. You would already be a moderate risk taker (as were the servants with three and five talents respectively). You would not be like the "wicked servant", who was overly obsessed with self-preservation, and was unwilling to take even the slightest risk.

The first step to placing a demand on the economic system to affect your wealth transfer is recognizing and exercising your innate talents and skills.

This enabled God (Yahweh) to affect the first wealth transfer from Egypt through Joseph. It was Moses' experience and knowledge of Egyptian politics, as well as his connection to royal lineage himself, which helped to affect the second great Egyptian wealth transfer.

It was The United States' willingness to give, to rebuild Europe after the devastating Second World War (forsaking its previous policy of self-preservation and isolation), which enabled it to become the sole superpower nation on the planet. It was China's enviable large population and work ethic, which enabled it to affect a great wealth transfer from The United States. It will be the new wealthy of America (Generation X millionaires), which will affect a return to America's dominance in manufacturing and overall productivity.

The first step in understanding your talents, skills, and opportunities is to conduct a SWOT. This is a technique that Marketers, Business and Investment Analysts use, to identify a firm's full market potential.

We must remember that we live in a free market, capitalist oriented economy. God (Yahweh) at this time will use that system to affect a wealth transfer to you, as he used the agrarian based command economy of Egypt to affect the great wealth transfers to Israel.

SWOT stands for Strengths, Weaknesses, Opportunities, and Threats.

In this chapter the reader will be given information on how to perform a personal SWOT analysis, to identify skills, talents, and abilities. The reader will then be given techniques for looking at self-weaknesses and threats that have been militating against these strengths and opportunities.

Following the SWOT, the reader will be given techniques and strategies to identify their "top three" strengths and opportunities that have the potential to place a demand on the economy to affect a wealth transfer.

Readers will be taught techniques for identifying problems around them and posing solutions to these problems from the reservoir of personal skills, aptitudes, competencies, and abilities identified in the SWOT. Practical examples will be given of actual wealthy persons who used their innate, God (Yahweh) talent, skills, and abilities. These persons used "what was in their hands" to place a demand on Egypt to transfer wealth to them so to speak.

These wealthy people found practical solutions to the problems other people were having. Such persons include in the modern world, Elon Musk Founder of PayPal and SpaceX in California, and Facebook founders John Zuckerburg (a college dropout), Dustin Moskowitz et al.

These wealthy entrepreneurs are constantly in search of opportunities, not falling into the rich trap of self-preservation. They want to impact the world in multiple ways.

Opportunities for wealth transfers exist in publishing, product development, management problem solving, health and wellness, fitness, and technology, just to name a few.

In this chapter, the reader will understand the opportunities for wealth transfer in "the better mouse trap" principle, backed by Godly principles.

CHAPTER TEN: STORIES OF DIVINE WEALTH TRANSFER

Wealth transfer isn't just about sudden financial gain or inherited riches. Often, it is the result of divine strategy—using what you already have in your hands. These are the stories of four individuals, each with humble beginnings, who experienced personal wealth transfer by tapping into their God-given talents, refining their skills, and seizing life-changing opportunities.

Danielle: The Teacher Who Became a Curriculum Queen

Danielle was a quiet primary school teacher in a small island town. She loved children, but her paycheck barely covered her expenses. Yet, she had a gift—she could simplify complex topics and create colorful, fun learning tools that her students adored.

One day, a visiting education officer noticed her vibrant classroom charts and asked if she could make some for other teachers. That simple request opened a door. Before long,

Danielle was designing digital educational materials and selling learning kits to schools across the island chain.

Eventually, she transitioned out of the classroom and built a full-time business developing curriculums, hosting teacher workshops, and equipping schools with tools to elevate

Learning. Her gift for teaching became a global tool for transformation—and a source of financial overflow.

Her oil was teaching. Her vessels were schools. Her wealth transfer came when she recognized the opportunity and poured out her gift.

Kevin: The Mechanic Who Built a Mobile Empire

Kevin had golden hands—he could fix anything with an engine. After years of working at a garage for modest pay, he decided to offer mobile services on weekends to busy professionals and elderly clients who couldn't leave their homes. Word spread quickly.

But Kevin didn't stop at success—he multiplied it. Instead of turning away extra work, he trained two young men from his community. In time, he built a team, bought a few branded vans, and created Kev's Mobile Mechanics—a full-service mobile operation serving the entire region.

Kevin didn't need a storefront or a fancy degree. He turned his hands-on skill into a thriving business that not only blessed his family but also created employment for others.

His skill became a stream. His hustle became a harvest. His impact became his increase.

Aaliyah: The Seamstress Who Sewed Her Way into Destiny

Aaliyah's journey started at her grandmother's sewing machine. For years, she mended clothes and made simple dresses for neighbors and church members. She never charged much—just enough to buy more fabric. But within her was a dream for something greater.

That dream took a turn when a local influencer asked her to design a custom outfit for a women's conference. Aaliyah gave it her all. When the outfit hit social media, her inbox lit up. The demand for her bold, elegant designs exploded overnight.

She soon launched her own fashion label, began shipping internationally, and started hosting online sewing classes to empower other aspiring designers. What started as a hidden hobby became a global fashion and empowerment brand.

Her opportunity came wrapped in a one-time request. But her readiness met the moment. Today, her business is more than fashion—it's ministry.

Jaz Chipman: From the Sandlot to the Stadium

Raised in The Bahamas, Jaz Chipman spent much of his childhood trailing behind his grandmother at the local softball park. He watched the games closely, mimicking every swing in his imagination. Though too young to play, he became the unofficial

Helper, fetching balls, cleaning the dugout, and doing whatever he could just to be near the game.

Eventually, someone noticed his determination and invited him to join a small community baseball team. That was all the spark he needed. Jaz trained hard, absorbed every coaching tip, and played with heart and hustle.

With each level he climbed—from local games to national showcases—his name grew. Today, Jaz Chipman is one of the top baseball players for the New York Yankees, representing not only his talent but his nation on the world stage.

His journey began in the dirt and dust of a neighborhood field, fueled by discipline and destiny. He never stopped believing.

"Never despise small beginnings. I started as a ball boy at a local park. But I showed up every day like I was already on the team. Your attitude toward your small start determines how far your talent will take you." —Jaz Chipman

Each of these individuals had something in their hand: a skill, a passion, a gift. What made the difference was their willingness to invest in it, serve with it, and trust God to open the right doors.

Danielle's classroom turned into a company Kevin's garage experience turned into a fleet. Aaliyah's sewing became a global style ministry.

Jaz's grit on the sidelines became greatness on the field.

Their stories remind us that wealth transfer is not about waiting—it's about working what God gave you until it works for you.

So, what's in your hand?

BIBLIOGRAPHY

Barker, Kenneth, Burdick, Donald, Hindson, Edward; Mitchell, Daniel; Stek, John; Wessel, Walter; Youngblood, Ronald; Zondervan, King James Version, Study Bible, Zondervan Publishing, Grand Rapids, 2002.

Bahr, Lauren S.; Johnston, Bernard; P.F. Collier L.P., New York, 1993.

www.business.time.com/2013/07/24/whatitmeanstobewealthyinameri ca today

www.wsj.com/articles

ABOUT THE AUTHOR

This book was conceptualized by (Late) Mr. Keith Dean who was a financial advisor. He was also a lecturer in accounting and entrepreneurship. He has a passion for helping others unlock their potential. Keith started writing this book, but was unable to complete it. This book, Nurturing Your Wealth Transfer, was revised and completed by Dr. Larriett Josey Dean. Dr. Larriett is a Social and Counseling psychologist and Life Coach, who is essentially interested in helping people to evolve, unlock their potential and live the best version of themselves, while fulfilling their God given purpose.

Made in the USA
Monee, IL
04 November 2026

67386537R00036